The Fly in the Ointment

The Fly in the Ointment

TWENTIETH-ANNIVERSARY EDITION

POEMS BY   Barrymore Ashe

Joseph Harrison

Frank Hart

Vironique

Stephen Wallace

EDITED AND WITH A PREFACE BY

J. H. Hobson

SYLLABIC PRESS

BALTIMORE, MARYLAND

ISBN 13: 978-0-692-32943-6

Syllabic Press

Syllabic Press
200 E. Joppa Road, Suite L-101
Towson, MD 21286
syllabicpress@gmail.com

Library of Congress Card No. 2014922131

I neglect God and all his angels for the noise of a fly

DONNE

the fly with all the long joys of summer before it

BECKETT

Contents

Preface

Though there was general agreement among the friends of Barrymore Ashe that something should be done to commemorate the 20th anniversary of his death, there was much discussion of what form this should take. A selection of his own poems, including the twenty-five that were in his final version of *The Fly in the Ointment*, plus, perhaps, a few of his poems from earlier stages of the project, might have seemed the most fitting tribute. But Ashe was quite specific about not wanting his poems to appear apart from the poems of his collaborators. *The Fly in the Ointment* was a collective project, an anthology Ashe put together combining his own poems with those of four friends, fully intending to call into question the accepted model of authorship. He made it clear, to numerous listeners on numerous occasions, that he did not believe "poems" could be said to be by "people" in any meaningful sense. A composition in numerous voices, at play with each other (and Ashe and his friends often worked together quite closely), could achieve every bit as much aesthetic unity and coherence as a volume arranged by a "single author," and would have the advantages of multivocality.

So it was agreed, almost unanimously, that we should do what Barrymore Ashe would probably have wished: publish *The Fly in the Ointment* in the form in which he left it at the time of his death in August of 1994. That book, of course, had taken multiple forms: Ashe put out no fewer than six versions of it between June 1992 and May 1994 from his own Gone Tomorrow Press (the only other volume that press printed was the single quite limited edition of *Shape's Horse*, in March 1994). Ashe seems to have considered the May 1994 version the final one, and the admission that he previously considered earlier versions of this ever-morphing book "final" does nothing to change the fact that this was his last arrangement of it. I have, with some reluctance, decided to make two changes to the form in which he left the book, which I will explain below. But first, since it is twenty years (hard to believe!) since Barrymore Ashe was among us, and this book may have readers too young to remember him, or even to have heard of him, it might be wise to reestablish the once familiar facts.

The Fly in the Ointment grew out of the work of a performance poetry troupe called Fly, organized by Ashe, that gave frequent readings in the poetry cafes of Baltimore, and occasionally elsewhere, between 1989 and 1994. Originally the group consisted of, along with Ashe, Joseph Harrison, Frank Hart, and Stephen Wallace. Harrison dropped out at the end of 1989, and Hart's participation was sporadic throughout, depending on whether or not he had anything new to contribute. For a period of about a year, Fly was essentially Barrymore Ashe and Stephen Wallace. Then, in the spring of 1992, Ashe began a multimedia collaborative venture entitled Shape's Horse with the artist who then went by the name Vironique, and Vironique joined Fly as well. Wallace left the group near the end of 1992; Harrison rejoined early in 1993; when the group gave its final series of performances in the spring of 1994, it included Ashe, Harrison, Hart, and Vironique.

I mention all this because it partially determines the structure of *The Fly in the Ointment*. The arrangement of the book is roughly chronological, and Ashe took great care to place in proximity the poems written and revised in dialogue with each other, then performed together. So, for instance, Ashe's "Poetry" and "The Origins of Poetry" are followed by Wallace's "Legend" and Hart's "Ode": all four were part of a "set" memorably performed by Fly at several venues, most notably at the Cafe MonTage in Baltimore in November of 1991. *The Fly in the Ointment* is not a chronicle of the evolution of Fly: a truly inclusive document, including all the pieces performed (and Ashe kept precise records of this) would run to several times the length of this volume, and would prove unwieldy, however interesting to historians of the American poetic avant-garde. Ashe had, moreover, a good sense of which poems were the best ones, and the cuts he made over the years to the evolving book seem generally in the right. But the trajectory of the book does follow the trajectory of the troupe, and this seems worth keeping in mind.

I have made only one change in the sequence as Ashe left it. The final version begins with Harrison's poem "R. M. H.," and does not include his poem "Frost Heaves." Most previous versions of *The Fly in the Ointment,* including the penultimate one, printed in January of 1994, began with "Frost Heaves," and did not include "R. M. H." But soon after the January version was produced (in small numbers, as always) Harrison asked Ashe to remove "Frost Heaves" from any future editions, since the poem had been accepted by a magazine, but was not scheduled to appear for a year, and Harrison did not wish to forego the magazine publication. Harrison offered "R. M. H." as a replacement, which Ashe eventually accepted. But Harrison has reminded me that Ashe was not, initially, at all happy about this change, and I, too, recall him being displeased at this, and feeling that (a) "Frost Heaves" was a stronger beginning to the book; and (b) as it had been read at all the most important early performances of Fly, which "R. M. H." had not, it had the better claim to stand at the front. (Ashe also told me that he believed Harrison was being both unnecessarily punctilious in this matter, and self-contradictory: the magazine in question was highly unlikely to be aware of Ashe's small press, and the poem had already appeared in several earlier versions of *The Fly in the Ointment.*) Since the copyright issues no longer pertain, Harrison has suggested dropping "R. M. H." and replacing it with "Frost Heaves," as he believes Ashe would have wished. Though he may well be right about this, I felt that if I were to be true to my purpose, to reproduce the book as Ashe left it, I should not be dropping poems. So I have decided, over Mr. Harrison's objection, on a compromise measure, printing "R. M. H." first, as an "alternate" beginning (bracketed in the table of contents), then "Frost Heaves," followed by the poems ("The Painter's Portrait," "The Fly," and "The New Writing") it was so frequently performed with.

I should also note, in deference to Mr. Harrison, that I have overridden his wishes with respect to two other matters. He did not want to see the poem "Scylla and Charybdis" included, as he no longer cares for it. But he signed the copyright on the poem over to Ashe, and I, as Ashe's literary executor, have the final say in this matter, and have decided that as Ashe included it it should go in. Harrison also asked me to restore the ending of the January 1994 version of the manuscript, which did not conclude with Harrison's poem "Ivan Ho," but followed "Ivan Ho" with Ashe's own "Adam" and "In the Ointment," thus giving Ashe the last word. As appropriate as this might seem, Ashe chose to drop "In the Ointment" and to put "Ivan Ho" last in his final version, and this was just one of many changes the May 1994 version made to the January one. The May version included no new poems (other than "R. M. H."), but did extensive cutting, and some reordering, and I have decided to remain faithful to those choices.

The other change I have made with even greater reluctance. Ashe, quite deliberately of course, did not identify the authors of the poems in any of the editions he printed, as he wished the book's "voices" to blend together as much as possible. And I have excluded the names of the authors from the text proper, if you will. But, given the value of the book as historical document, and as tribute to Ashe, I thought it appropriate to let the reader see what poem was by which contributor (not that it isn't apparent enough without the identification). One possibility was to include the information in a note, but little enraged Ashe more than the inclusion of "notes" at the end of books of poetry, which he bemoaned as yet another sign of the "neutering ossification of the art within the academy," as he once put it. (I have little doubt this preface itself would enrage him.) So I have included the authors' names in the table of contents, with apologies to his ghost.

J. H. HOBSON

The Fly in the Ointment

R. M. H.

A slow elegant bass voice—my father's?
Not quite. The roll, the pause, the sweet, firm kiss
Of irony—my Uncle Robert's—gone.

With his unique experience of the world,
Songbirds and scalding zones and growing seasons,
Bright desert flowers, striped sandstone formations,
Dust storms and freshets, winter constellations . . .

The silver names snap off and drop unspoken.
An old man lays his head against a stone.
The breath a boy struggled for in Virginia,
Seized in the fierce air of the desert, gone,

An echo in the voice of my father
Crying into the darkness of the phone.

Frost Heaves

"Harrison loves my country too,
But wants it all made over new."

In a diminished corner of New England,
Between two pummeled spines of the Green Mountains,
You'll find a town and college, Middlebury,
That once were haunts of the poet, Robert Frost.
He's honored ways some dead would find offensive.
Just read the markers on the road to Randolph
Where the new writers come and go like leaves:
You cross the Robert Frost Memorial Bridge
To see, on the Robert Frost Memorial Drive,
The Robert Frost Interpretive Nature Trail,
The Robert Frost Memorial Wayside Area,
And then a crooked stick-sign, with crude letters,
Warning of shocks from shifty weather: FROST HEAVES.

And who could blame you, pseudo-memorialized
So comically in every wrong direction
Like any Vince Lombardi or Joyce Kilmer?
Or should we rather blame that side of you
Who packaged your keen words like maple syrup,
Dripping with smug provinciality,
Sticky with rhyme? As if you never contrived
To warp the ripe world through thin panes of ice,
Or plotted the marshy ground in fours and fives
Crisp to the cut of your long whispering scythe,
Or started the couple arguing on the stairs,
The narrow, clumsy, stoic will defied
By love's white backward gaze of grief at loss
Till call by liquid call the songbirds changed,
Or hid the goblet behind the children's playhouse.

4

And now it seems you've gotten me lost again
Although I thought I knew these woods by heart:
Splashes of yellow and alizarin,
Pulse of magenta, every fist in flame.
Something coaxes the trees to dress themselves
In the last colors of the alphabet
Then strips them in the nick of the north wind,
Something crisps the trail, ices the bridge,
Encrusts the plaque in the wayside area
And hoists the pavement, buckling it like clay.
Long after your crumbling image is forgotten
(Beside the hero on inauguration day)
Frost will wrestle stone from underneath
And crack our polished, placid surfaces,
Wrenching apart the road we thought we'd taken.

The Painter's Portrait

For minutes of eternity,
Juan de Pareja,
Your eyes

Insist it no simple
Appearance
You are alive.

> *"the master has so captured . . . his friends were astonished . . .*
> *could not distinguish the portrait . . . the original"*

Stand close the illusion
Hangs on the wall,
Another painting,

Retreat your stare
Steps into focus,
Follows.

How many faces
Have you witnessed
Disappear

From your pose
At the cusp
Of time?

How few suspect
Your secret?
Does Palomino?

> *"A native of Seville, mestizo by birth, and of odd color. He was*
> *the slave of Don Diego Velazquez, and although his master*
> *(for the honor of art) never allowed him to assist in anything*
> *having to do with painting or drawing, but permitted him*
> *only to grind colors and from time to time prime a canvas and*

do other chores about the studio and house, he performed these
with such skill that, unbeknownst to his master, and stealing
hours while he was sleeping, he eventually made paintings
well worthy of esteem."

And hid one
Among the master's.
The king declared:

>"A painter of such abilities must not be a slave."

"Emanc.1651," you
Stayed with Velazquez,
His daughter after.

Elsewhere the master painted
The constipated nobility,
The humiliated dwarf.

But here with exact gravity
To his good trusted hand
What has he done?

>*"One becomes almost conscious of the presence of some sentient*
>*thing, imploring our attention, as if it lived only in that brief*
>*span."*

A life not life,
No blood but in those dark eyes
Some speed of light, of mind . . .

>*"the essence of the soul . . . trapped . . . immortal"*

His strokes

Your gaze

The Fly

To an animal, the fly is a fly.
An animal will eat a fly or, ignored, the fly flies away.
But I am a human, I live in an apartment.
The fly is trapped in my apartment.

I can't write because the fly distracts me.
Crazy against the light the fly distracts me.
The fly is trapped in my apartment and may die here.
The fly is enormous.

I turn on the news, the President looks silly.
I don't care what happens to the fly.
The idea of the apartment was to live alone.
I wanted to be free in private pleasure.
I will kill the fly.

Something has happened in El Salvador.
There are bodies in the streets of the capital.
The Secretary of State is in my apartment, explaining.
I see enormous ears, a suit, a tie.
I see the fly.

An animal would eat the fly, or ignore it.

I am not an animal, I must free it.

I must free it for the sake of the apartment.

I turn off the news and the fly returns.

I start to write but there is the fly.

Crazy against the light the fly the fly

The New Writing

Click, squiggle, beep:
The purr of the machine's
Consent, programmed and unafraid,
A maiden space expansive as spangled
Galaxies, microscopic as the cell
Positioned in its pocket now unspools
To be fashioned in all wise and form
And all are welcome, yes, come in, come in,
The dancing has just started, the floors
Click and shine, the grouped guests sparkle,
All disapproving widows are asleep
And children too, there is no childhood here
Just innocence and ribbons and balloons
And a fat man farting and chuckling,
Drunk in the corner. Tippling he rises,
Greets you, brims your glass, begins a joke
When the perfume of the hostess intercedes
And jeweled fingers fastened to your sleeve
Lead you to the balustrade where you see her:
Shy at the dance, unspoken for, the new muse,
Diminutive synthetic graces wait
Attendant on each touch of tip to key,
Her dark hair tucked back her earrings
Catch the scintillations of the chandeliers
As she lingers by the fruit tray, eating grapes.

Local History

When you see how one builds his house of clay and sticks, another
    of bones and feathers, then you wonder.

The governess scolded the children till they cried.

Rules were important in the pristine village, shoes were essential.

When children died their families kept their shoes.

String, cloth, and seven railroad ties; plywood and old tires; a contrap-
    tion of shoe boxes, broomsticks, and wires.

The children were told stories of the dump, histories of the village,
    none of them true.

There was a palace with parquet floors and a thousand and one
    mirrors.

There was a labyrinthine gymnasium built solely with two-by-fives.

There was a gallery with portraits of the universal human truths.

The governess scolded the children till they cried.

They had been to see for themselves, their shoes were muddy.

Canvas and pieces of sewer pipe; four former Christmas trees and
    charred rope; a few dozen books from the village library, long
    closed.

And the shrunken, chattering shamans, piecing the world together,
    buzzed on wine.

Poetry

It seems to frighten people when you say it.

At a street corner, or on a bus, in a diner, or during a cocktail party.

People look at you like you're crazy, crazy to do that.

No one listens to what you're saying, you make them uneasy.

They hurry by, get off, pay up, go look for Frederick.

A woman politely tries to persuade you to stop.

But it's what you like to do and you keep doing it.

A man in a suit angrily demands that you shut up.

"We've heard enough of this shit!" he shouts, "Enough of this shit!"

But it's the middle of the first book of your epic,

The doomed hero's exhorting his companions.

Someone seems to have summoned the police.

The hero sings out, "Let's fight like cornered wolves!"

Suddenly furious, the police beat you.

The people applaud as they drag your mouth away.

"He was a nut," they mutter, "he was a crazy."

The Origins of Poetry

It began with the recognition that he was "insane."

Now everything was possible, trees were his allies, and the moon.

And the bugs make little noises.

A songbird starts up, follow the pretty songbird.

Is someone watching?

Someone, a god?

Does someone want to play, play in the garden?

In the garden there are people playing golf.

Hit the ball, hit the ball down the pretty fairways.

Drive, chip, and putt, drive, chip, and putt.

He wrecked the golf cart

Wrote the wrong score and stole the wingtip shoes

Legend

Each minute lifts the figure of itself.
Bonfires gutter to ash, their lingering scrawl
And elegy dissolves. The sky proceeds
With a color as immaculate, unique,
And free of cloud as pure transparent blue.

And within a tuft of weeds the pale blue egg:
To find a delicate image of the world,
To cup it in your hands, and think the snake
Would find its meat delicious, yes, and greed
Vibrate his gullet's pulse and narrow view . . .

To swear the curse that halts him, and replace
Undisturbed its fragile possible life,
To have the eye enjoy but not intrude
We desire and need but did not know. The bird
Won't touch her young if we have, and we have.

The ape broke into the garden and ran wild.
He smeared each fruit and flower with a name
And since he owned each name he owned each thing.
His word, his word, his word: he danced and laughed
And drank its sweet concoctions until ill.

The cautionary history of the world,
With evidence and color illustrations,
Appears too late. Professor X has quibbles,
The President laughs on the golf course, the crowd
Leaves, happy the long tournament is over.

They muddled the grim legend, the old fathers,
Mistaking prophecy for history.
This was paradise, foreign to the primate
And the engines of his fingers and his will
Who fouls his own nest and devours his children.

Ode

Walked the shore,
The fractal of the sea's
White margin wavering
A stripe of sand.

Inches from two bare feet
The creep, recede,
Stretch and collapse,
Frothing and hissing in.

Printing a broken line
The feet stay almost dry,
The water just ahead
Or just behind

Each footstep measuring
The trembling edge
Of the old distinction,
Sea and land.

The course of all long journeys,
Risk and luck,
A faith in elements
Barely justified

As pure need to believe
They are benign,
If just this day, this hour,
They are kind . . .

And the torn weeds run
Slinging sand,
Cassiopeia
Clears the rim of the sky.

The great terns,
Hungry, hooded,
Rise and cry
Sea, sea,

Feed, feed,
Curve high in the brisk
And pivot,
Sea, sea, sea.

Tomorrow would bring his contest with the sun.

———————————

Limiting
Exposure
Limit pain
And limit pleasure.

The sand is light,
The waves are light,
Throbbing in the eyes
And skull.

The poor pale flesh
As sacrifice
To sun's insistent
Lash and calculus:

No ointment
Is so permanent
The light can't tear
Its coat in time,

Timing is essential,
And a feel

For sensing pain
Before the point of pain.

Dangerous extremity,
A game
Against a gladiator
Who does not lose

Played by one
Foolish and afraid
Of things that limit
Character and skill:

Stride on, though deep sand blunts the stride.

———————————

Till all but asleep
In the roll and swell,
The slender shore
Reappearing,

Nerve filaments quiet,
Muscles smooth,
The crisp salt
Cool at each pore,

And the blood in pulse
With the huge heart
And cradle,
Ancient and animal,

Slow rhythm
Of origin,
Almost asleep
In the soft drift and fall . . .

While the white belly scalds.

———————

Night the wind
Slams Hatteras,
All down the island
Lights cut down.

Massive over Avon
The sky cracks,
Flimsy staggered cabins
Lurch in the flash.

There's fear
In every photograph,
The frailty
Of all we frame,

The folly of building
By the sea.
And terror
At the total dark between,

Stuck on this severed
Finger of sand,
Open to the size
Of sky and ocean,

Still, morning stood, stilts planted in pools of rain.

New Hoyle & Improved

The best part of making up games is inventing odd rules.

Like everything has to fit in one straight line.

Or the right hand always has to be touching wood.

Or you can only win by one.

Or the ball has to hit Billy's head before it goes in.

The rules make the game fun, or hard, or hilariously impossible
     to complete.

For a moment it doesn't matter who wins.

We're all ridiculous, incompetent.

The rules win, it's their game and they're just too good.

Then someone cheats, or falls, or Billy quits.

It was fun while it lasted, original fun.

Interview

What time frame?

The narrative of a life, a series of employment opportunities.

Who's profited from your labor, will they recommend you?

Doodling on the application.

Just try and explain to the receptionist, face caked and big hair.

Or her boss, stress city and fresh from pastrami.

"Value" a trap door, the hidden agenda.

And who may infiltrate their operation?

Little acts of sabotage.

A weird rumor about one of the managers.

A nasty form letter to a wealthy customer.

Then seize the podium at the company meeting.

To tell them about time, about money and time.

About all the useless time wasted in useless jobs.

All for golf.

For a receding idea of the good life.

Or because their father told them: "Get a job."

Hapax

Out of all context, singular and strange,
The indefinable original,
Pure printless entry in a lexicon
Rubbed clean of limitation and precision,
Grammar's conditioned rule and logic's flaw.

This meant some thing perhaps, a child's bright toy,
A garden tool or household instrument
For cooking or for measuring the weather,
Or a puzzle, a predicament, a mood,
A rhetorician's gamble, twisted in play.

Erosion of its world renders a nut
And cipher, empty in significance,
Figuring the gradual disturbance
Of the whole webbed and fading edifice
Through time, the slow galactic turbulence.

They named the constellations once: then
Chaos seemed delimited by order.
Lines connected the stars, a dog appeared,
A bear. The hemispheres took character
And purpose, one vast radiant form.

Advocates of astrology contend
Of influence unseen yet permanent,
The color of a footstep, of a room,
A tissue of accretive interest
To which apparent wanderings conform,

But this ignores all circumstance, and stands
Assured in its uncertainty, obscure
As the mysterious thin frequency
Emitted by the field that hummed and whirred
Before the explosion of the visible world.

King Arthur

So he was the king, it was supposed to be a big deal.

But he took a dump in the morning just like anybody.

And no he wasn't quick as he used to be.

Years of flattery, servility.

Even the good friends docile, obedient.

When was the last time he'd had a real conversation?

Who wants to tell a king what's on their mind?

And Guinevere was fucking Lancelot.

He tried to believe she wasn't.

Couldn't stop thinking about it.

In her chambers, every afternoon.

She was difficult to read but he was obvious.

How many before Lance?—he could think of a few.

Had everyone been laughing at him all along?

Losing the sword was bad, but this was worse.

In her chambers, every afternoon,

The goddamned Frenchman and his beautiful queen.

Vertical Invasion

From a trap door in the center of the stage pops the demented naif.

He is dressed like Picasso, but carrying golf clubs.

He jokes in a foreign language, the crowd is puzzled.

He takes a book from his right pocket and reads in blurred, uncertain English: a dictionary.

He takes a paper from his left pocket and reads a series of numbers, ambiguous statistics.

A couple in the third row rises to leave.

He pulls a driver from the golf bag and plants a tee.

Was that bucket of golf balls there before?

Shots whip into the crowd. Laughter, then panic: real golf balls.

One nails the man who was leaving on the ear.

Someone's front teeth broken, a cheek smashed.

Everyone pushing and running.

But the doors of the auditorium are locked.

"He's got a gun!" a woman screams, "he's got a gun!"

Cotton Mather Singing

Forgot the steeple bells, and when the blue
Of afternoon brought cloud forms did not call
On Latin names or kabbalistic charms.
A world unbroken in each stride of light,
Wide fields of water shivered and grew calm.

He found the name, traditional and strange,
Some doomed enthusiast grimly possessed
By visions of eternity, and called
From mean conviction and self-righteousness
To thump time on a rickety pulpit.

That was Cotton Mather, that was the hat
That gripped his head. He wore it to his grave
And in his grave the hat became his child.
He told it stories, pilgrimage and food
Or dozing by the fire, the sermon done.

And when the hat grew up a loud guitar
It rollicked as it strummed a rumpled brood.
Thrashing voltage slammed the battered words
At crashing decibel, all syllable
And tone lost in the blasted neon air.

The signs of love grew larger. Cotton wept
And sings the comic truth, god is a small
Child in a biblical painting by Chagall,
Who laughs at the castle of blocks knocked down
Or storms and howls, frustrated and inept.

The dancers on the dance floor do not care
What Cotton Mather didn't eat or why.
Desire turns each season, late at night
Encroachments on our sleep morph into form
With the guitarist's bold familiar chords.

Orpheus

After all that he lost her.
He never knew quite how, he made up the stories.
Singing to win her back in front of all Hades.
He did sing down there, but it wasn't like that.
He couldn't tell what they thought, they seemed puzzled.
A man singing his grief at his lover's death to the dead.
It wasn't relevant.

But Eurydice liked it, and said she'd come back.
She remembered enough of life to desire its pleasures.
She might try again.
It wasn't clear what happened next, they were going out,
He looked at her anxiously or spoke in the wrong tone.
Or it was something else entirely.
But she was gone.

The Head of Orpheus

Something traumatic had certainly been erased.

It half-remembered the body, other bodies.

The eloquent music.

But screaming drowns the music and memory stops.

Some thing will not admit mutilation.

A fearful wall.

Then water, river, waves.

Schools of trigger fish noticing coral caves.

Now things were easier, a head on the sand.

Birds, wind, seaweed, occasional rain.

No other noise to counter the gathering voice.

It sang the new song again.

A Bird

      the wind

           ride

              the wind

A Girl

      ribbon

           hair

     neck

knee

A Mountain

tip

Geography Zero

Where?
They didn't know and didn't care.
Uncool, dude.
School.
The foolish teacher, bored.

What dead where?
Over there, man, over there.

Coach Jesus

When you want to win so bad you'd die for it.

That's when you're ready to play for Coach Jesus.

Just another high school football coach.

Metal plate in his head.

And Jesus in the locker room before each game.

When you won it was him, it was Jesus.

When you lost it was you.

Laps.

Coming back from the accident made him a leader of men.

He was a coach, like God.

Sending the injured player back in the game.

"Gotta just play through the pain, boy.

Jesus died for your soul, boy, you can stand pain."

He crippled the boy, he won the game.

Now he's a hero, Coach Jesus.

Someone Else's Hat

Ever thought of someone else's hat?
On your head.
The fear of looking ridiculous, the jibes.
"You're not Thomas Jefferson!"

But why not?
He had a hat, a head.
The head wanted a gardener who could play the French horn.
The hat cocked for the ladies.

Politics was literary, personal.
"You've thrown me out!" snapped Adams, "thrown me out!"
But on the fiftieth: "Thomas Jefferson still lives."
You listening in the ether, "dead."

Violin

we

wee

we

we

swee'

sweep

weep

sweep

weep

Train of Thought

So what was the point of all this?

News every morning and evening, news with food.

At night the world domination dreams.

The countries of the world in alphabetical order: Afghanistan, Albania, Algeria, Andorra.

Different people eat different food, no chef cooks in all the styles.

But what if one did, and opened a restaurant?

Eggplant in yogurt sauce, lamb shish kebab, chicken tangine with seven vegetables over couscous.

Many people would think it dumb compared to McDonald's.

Some would want to go but never get there, never get to Baltimore.

Bangor, Baton Rouge, Battle Creek, Bay City.

What if a million Czechs moved to an American city and elected a poet mayor?

He would rewrite its laws in verse, beautiful but difficult to understand.

He would sneak in private jokes and conundrums.

Lawyers would be forced to study poetry.

Some passages would be clarified, but much remains bewildering.

And the people love their poet mayor, because he's poor like them and says funny things.

Then he announces his candidacy for Vice-President.

It isn't even an election year.

But the incumbent is an embarrassment, a poll shows the poet ahead.

Petitions are submitted demanding a special election.

The Vice President addresses a Kiwanis convention.

He babbles helplessly, handlers lead him offstage.

The President says nothing, Congress is confused.

The Supreme Court rules poetry obscene, the poet is arrested.

But the people riot in all the cities.

Commerce, Concord, Coon Rapids, Coral Gables.

They barricade parking lots and seize shopping malls.

The government falls, the poet takes over.

Vice President of the United States of America.

Colfax, Wilson, Wheeler, Arthur.

Vice President of America, with no President.

This probably couldn't happen.

It's just an example of how things might be different.

A lot of people in this country have a bum deal.

Let's all just agree to scramble the deck and start over.

Seven card high-low, Jacks wild low, deuces high.

Got it?

Just play along, you'll pick it up eventually.

If you're feeling lucky risk your money.

Or we'll play something else.

Everyone gets someone else's hand, you get Dan Rather's.

He takes your job as a clerk in a bookstore or a teaching assistant, you take his.

Every night you report the world to millions.

You describe poverty, war, and oppression in Africa, Asia, and Latin America.

You descry the crimes of greedy exploitation, you make fun of the President.

But Dan is depressed and bewildered.

He's bored at the store, or doesn't understand the books he's teaching.

He telephones, pleading with you to switch back.

What would you do?

Which is more important, informing the general public or books and students?

The cloistered life has its attractions, summers off, the smell of the familiar.

But the new life has power, the drug and danger of power.

The dream of your face on the screen . . .

Even as "the poetry guy" on channel 89.

People say, "Let's watch the poetry guy, there's nothing else on."

Auden, Blake, Crane, Donne, Eberhardt, Feldman, Googe.

The poetry guy can talk about anybody, he rattles off readings like sports facts.

He recites the old favorites.

The day's guest reads, an interview follows.

For seven years the show has a small but faithful audience.

Then metamorphosis of the national psyche.

Poetry becomes wildly popular, readings are thronged.

The private lives of poets turn tabloid fodder.

Teenage girls shriek and faint when poets read their trademark lines.

Skinheads start frequenting readings, adopting some poets as unwilling mentors.

They march around chanting, "In the middle of my life all things are white!"

The guardians of high culture lament its deterioration in eschatalogical rhetoric.

Poets are glad to have the extra money, but the pressure gets to some, there's a high burnout rate.

Your fanbase wants an album just like the last one, your critics don't.

Would this be an improvement?

I mean, poets complain about not having an audience, but do we really want one?

Of course we do, you have to admit we do.

Late at night, to the crinkled pillow, this is the tear-stained wish.

Not because we think we can save the world.

But as the stump of the left arm remembers the severed wrist.

A place where, a day when poetry mattered.

(It still does some places today, but never here, a tampering executive
would make my day.)

Not that it hasn't remained limber and apt.

Not that it doesn't express the historical moment.

But it cannot address that moment, the great wind machine slams our
puny voices back down our throats.

And lament for this state of affairs echoes throughout the unhappy
valley.

What we were when we were what we were, the original verb.

The fire the hero brought us, stolen from gods, words for the rising
sun.

The new world they lit and warmed.

From this lie philosophy's truth and history's story, religion's uncon-
scious lie.

And the squat clay huts rose by the river, the fields took form.

At night, by the fire, the bright musical stories, the dancing.

The held hands, the quick pulse of a common song.

If this never happened it's been imagined often.

Thus the kneejerk of self-righteousness, the importance of poetry.

But this is America.

An actor in a television series, a backup quarterback, a personality.

Fred would rather meet them than any poet.

Have them over for barbecue, or maybe just go for beers.

Fred knows a poet, named Marvin.

Marvin doesn't actually write poetry.

But he thinks a lot, is moody, says weird things, has lots of schemes.

Phyllis, who runs the office, says this makes him a poet.

He's not a bad guy, or he wasn't.

But when he snapped he snapped good.

Holding the gun to the head of the branch manager.

It wasn't money he wanted, it was publicity.

Publicity for his cause, except he didn't have one.

And he wouldn't surrender until he figured one out.

"The rain forest!" he shouted, "divestment from South Africa! the homeless!"

Something had to be done about these problems.

"I'm a poet!" he screamed, "a poet and terrorist!"

"I'm the Siamese Liberation Army!"

It made the papers and news shows three days in a row.

CRAZED POET HOLDS HOSTAGE IN BANK

TENSE STANDOFF IN CLEVELAND CONTINUES

POET DEMANDS SPACE TELESCOPE BE REPAIRED

The branch manager collapsed, so Marvin released him.

He tried to hold himself hostage but they shot him.

He was an OK fellow except for that.

And so it goes, in communities across the country.

Fayetteville, Fitchburg, Flagstaff, Flint, Florissant, Fond du Lac.

Things mostly quiet, then a crime, accident, or natural disaster.

An outpouring of public sympathy, a visit from the governor.

Then pretty much back to standard.

A news report on the anniversary of the occasion.

The people directly affected haven't completely recovered.

Phyllis still cries sometimes, the branch manager has trouble sleeping.

But the communities keep normalizing their relations.

Mansfield, Marion, McAllen, McKeesport.

If a fringe is excluded, that's just how it goes.

The price to be paid for the comfortable, bland fabric.

Naperville, Nashua, Nashville, National City.

Reruns of a sitcom, the same familiar shows.

So what's the problem?

That some places it isn't just a fringe?

That what you don't see is as important as what you see, and may be more real?

The hidden insults, the loss of the corner store.

The eradication of local prejudices by broader, national prejudices.

The rhetoric of national interest, the blatant whack of the flag.

The belief we have the right to lead the world.

We have a right to the sugar of the islands, the coffee of South America, the oil of Arabia.

And the right to enforce our will with a huge army.

And off we go to fight Saddam Hussein, evil enemy of the year for 1990.

Manuel Noriega won in 1989, Willie Horton the year before.

The world according to US, comfortable and simple.

For US.

But that was the twentieth century, which is nearly over.

Which began ending in 1989.

For now comes the close of the Age of the Great Nations,

The beginning of the time of the little countries.

A vast empire, our twin and opposite, crumbles to chaos.

And we are anxious, dangerous.

The Secretary of State is in my apartment again.

He says this is all about one thing and that's jobs.

The arms manufacturers' convention cheers the name of Saddam Hussein.

And war may boost the economy before the next election.

It's supposed to be bad form to mix politics and poetry.

But form isn't good or bad, it's functional.

And indistinguishable from what it carries.

An isolated line, a solipsistic nation.

Beating the war drums.

And I find this situation so distracting I cannot polish pretty things.

I keep hearing a noise, the mundane noise of news.

I keep seeing the crack in the mirror, the fly in the ointment.

But the President bombs Iraq, the nation cheers.

There's an electric change in our mood and weather.

The hourly crackle of war news.

Ordnance, smart bombs, collateral damage.

"We brought all our toys to the party," says the chief general.

And the war isn't just a just cause, a new crusade.

It's also a popular television show.

The night after the war begins I drive to Washington to teach a course in visionary poetry.

The capital is silent.

I take a wrong turn and wind up in front of the White House.

The President doesn't know I'm out here and doesn't care.

I'm sure he's more concerned with terrorists than poets.

It's true they pose a more immediate danger.

And he doesn't have much interest in long-term problems.

But he's a President, his memory will outlive him.

So perhaps it's poets he should really worry about.

Because now he's got me really angry at him.

This damned poem has gotten stuck right on his doorstep.

It was supposed to be a bigger poem than this, all about everything
else and then some.

But that light at the end of the tunnel is indeed a train.

And it's thundering down the track I'm puttering up.

What happens when poetry takes on history, just as it happens?

Takes it head on, at top speed?

The Persian Gulf War wrecks my train of thought.

Teacher

the student is always

                vulnerable

to judgment

                YOUR judgment

teacher

                a rigorous intelligence

                a blind, cruel heart

for their own good

                punishment

                humiliation

FOR THEIR OWN GOOD

                the goddess of necessity

    executes

———————————

you wanted disciples

                you seduced them

with mind not body

                (never BODY)

then

                FURIOUS REJECTION

for they must be broken

                for their own good

THEY MUST BE BROKEN FOR THEIR OWN GOOD

and remade

                as the OPPOSITE of their

      TEACHER

———————————

you loved my talents

                eye, ear, voice

and hated them

                you LOVED me, you HATED me

if I could be broken

if I could be broken . . .

I HAD to be BROKEN

                you TRIED to BREAK me

YOU TRIED TO BREAK ME

and failed

                did you fail?

———————————

teacher

          disenabling

for my own good

          I would not let you

I would not let YOU

          MANGLE me

I mangled myself

          to prevent you

———————

teacher

          the pain you inflicted

was gratuitous

          it was YOUR OBLIGATION

to HELP me

          (not rob me)

you failed

The Storm

                blew

                        and blew

low swirling yellow clouds

                        the new green trees

                        and blew

        dust and trash

                        birds off course

                        and blew

        disaster

                down the valley

                        wrecked the towns

        tossed the trailers

                        savage

                electric

                        weather

Night Song

The crazy rills of the mockingbird
In and out of the dreams
Throughout the night,

Light sweat on the bedclothes,
The sleeper half sleeper
Awake to the chronic worries,

Asleep in the song
Assaulting the tall curtained window
In mimic of agony,

The small bird's saxophone,

As if in and out of the dreams
Something outside
The conscious house we consciously secure

Told and told and told
What inside we unconsciously obscure
As the body obscures yet tells the spinal cord,

The sleeper straight up in bed like an open book,
The curtains alive in the light wind,
The light itself thin and fine,

The mockingbird tumbling scale on scale outside.

The Mischief

Everywhere it went it was the mischief.

The bug in the telephone, the knock in the throttle.

The little word the wrong way.

The terrible luck of meeting the Mortons there.

The elevator's stuck the elevator's stuck.

Nothing to do but stand helpless, stupid.

The frightened child shrieking.

The jerk.

Wedged into the postal box, the gift was crushed.

The jerryrigged car fix snapped on the interstate.

The old couple in the theater kept talking.

The wrong turn in Timonium.

We sat at the crossroads, laughing.

The riddle was anything.

Politics, the shape of the noise we live in.

The crack in the violin, the fly in the ointment.

Landscape with Snow Monsters

Trudging the edge of winter in Alaska.
The eye sees, heaped and humped, odd hillocks
Of snow. The sound of nothing crying
Echoes here as elsewhere, only more.
The stranger in this land does not imagine
Each drifted knoll of fallen crystal,
Dusted at random, fluted and folded,
Hides a coal. Those glittering pyramids
Do not melt (a thick, shagged rug shields them
From the heat of smelly oil's steady burn)
In the distant sun, they sit, still as if
Only a brilliant surface were present,
A cold blank mirror of the wintering mind,
When one will twitch and tremble, lift and crumble
Cascading from ascendant horns and thighs
And massive from its nap the musk ox rise.

Balboa

                saw

silent in his armor

                saw

                and knew

silent in his armor

                knew

                          the other side was water

                saw

                          the huge horizon

heavy armor

                isthmus

                          water always water

The Scholar Whose Library Burned

Woke up the next day. He was free. He'd tired
Of knowing too much, of reading too little.
His sorrow was not being there to see
His charmed rooms crumble as the singing names
Curled from their colorful spines in the flames,
To hear at last the agon of voices
Escaping their flashing corpora, to turn
At the second the walls stood veils of fire
Stepped through by shadow shapes, no two the same,
And bid each ghost by its own killing name.

Another Elvis Impersonator

Preening for the foppish costume party.

Or crooning a sloppy set at the scuzzy lounge.

White bell bottoms, sequins, the big black slick.

Yes, he's worse than the original.

But the essential question isn't aesthetic.

In the spotlight power's more conferred than earned.

The yearnings of hillbilly women.

Diamond hope of the holler, star over the trailer park.

Silkscreen portraits and statuettes in Miss Bonnie's bar.

ELVIS LIVES, ELVIS RULES on the side of a Dempsey Dumpster.

(Or REX QUONDAM, REX FUTURUS in a poem.)

Presence exponential as its absence.

Miss Bonnie's faith in an encore, returned to sender.

"I know I'll see him again before I die."

And who's to say there won't be a second coming?

Who's to say there isn't a king?

John Quest

Now can you hear the cry, laced with desire?
The wind would tell, it would, it would. Until
Vast images of vacant spaces rise
And fall, a white ice-bound volcano towers
Above sea-clouds, or perpendicular
Drops the vertiginous desert canyon.

The tale of punished travel through such places,
Premonitions of adventure as a child,
The plan, the homemade horse, the faulty map,
Weather no book predicted, strange creatures
Imaginary and dangerous, the old
Man of the landscape, his frail offer to guide,

The meager meal at his hut, his quiet daughter,
Imprisonment and torture, midnight escape,
Oasis on oasis turned mirage,
How what survived to tell and the whole lie
Is told in every time and told again.
With every telling it becomes more plain

No vision can deliver you the palm
For shade on the pristine shore of the island bay,
The breeze of recollection, and the breath
To gather thoughts, mix in what can't be thoughts,
And a picture of some color in the mind
Concoct, exotic, smooth, the tropical drink.

                                              sea
                          the
                                          see
                  to
                              climbs
              that
                          street
          stone
                          thin
          the
                              line
              walls
                          white

          two

      Portugal

Old Photograph

Edwardian England, a fat man in a car,
Waves his bowler as he regally proceeds
Down the thronged avenue: a happy time,
With supper piping hot, and brandy after.

So here's to old what never was and is,
The king's round face reflected in the snifter.

Little Italy

Whatever you want to put in this shoe fits.

Fresh cut flowers and water, if you wish.

Flowers look pretty stupid in the shoe.

An umbrella looks better, at least that has a point.

Or put money in the shoe, it doesn't care.

Whatever the shoe wears fits it.

It runs off, happy to be a shoe.

And when it stops running at last, there it will sit.

A little Italy, with hills and trees.

Locum Tenens

You wanted a doctor but look who showed up instead.
Vaguely Indian, chanting what sounds like gibberish.
Burning a weed and blowing the smoke in your face.
Advising you to fast and hallucinate.

You wanted a priest but in his place you got this.
Dancing, gesticulating, gurgling.
Lighting a pipe and passing it to you.
Exhorting you to imagine your animal spirit.

You wanted a lawyer but got this lunatic.
Leaping in fiendish glee.
Howling a curse upon your enemy.
Summoning spirits to exact revenge.

You wanted a scholar but here's his substitute.
Versed in the hidden arts of no clear truth.
Conjuring the soft ancestral voices.
Singing all starless night to the whispering dead.

Jogging in Street Clothes

Let's say you are walking down the street.
A man comes up to you and asks you to listen.
He starts fervently reciting poems.
How would you get out of that situation?

You walk away but he walks with you.
Like he's your friend, your mentor, and your guide.
You start to run, in suit and dress shoes.
He trots alongside.

Then he's gone and you're running along alone.
Like running in a dream, but it isn't a dream.
Somewhere back there was something you should have known.
But the blocks float by, you're gaining speed.

And that's the problem with poetry in public.
Like jogging in street clothes, it seems eccentric,
Confusing one form with another function.
And your feet are hurting and you're miles from home.

Huck Finn

come

summer

the river

calls

tugging

the heart

float

float

past

St. Louis

Cairo

Memphis

descend

the long winding

mingled waters

slowly widening

come follow

the brown central

heartstream of America

Late Idyll

The factories' gases paint the setting skies
Brilliant, unnatural colors, swirls of neon
And nuclear pink, rising to bloom as freon
Tears at the heavens, dazing our shaded eyes,

While our ears thrum to radio frequencies,
Riding the waves of noise as in a dream,
Or hear, like the voice of some mountain stream,
The sewer waters rushing to the seas.

Neo Manifesto

Fuck off, fathead!

Angry young men will run things from now on.

We'll make theories to justify whatever we do.

Opposition will be proof of your pathetic corruption.

Your taste is a blockheaded puppet of the dominant culture.

You don't have the inner purity of the artist.

And the point isn't really what anyone paints or writes.

It's the conviction of integrity behind it.

So let's all line up behind this principle.

The principle of lining up behind it.

The line starts here, I'm first, my friend is second.

It's a pivotal moment in cultural history.

We'll carry this charter before us like a flag

As we march into battle against the other people.

The people who go to sleep when we attack them.

We have to wake them up before we can slay them.

Spontaneous Combustion

Steve caught on fire at the intersection.

Waiting for the light, he just ignited.

He'd been feeling strange for several days.

"It's like I'm on fire," he told his friend John, "I'm burning up!"

John didn't think much of it at the time.

His friend was always pissed, a ticked-off guy.

His nerves were wires.

Human stupidity made him want to explode.

The dumb mechanic kept dicking around with his car.

He was missing the meeting.

The shithead in the left lane didn't signal, he missed the light.

He sat there, steaming.

He noticed his elbow seemed to be on fire.

His flesh was burning all over, so were his clothes.

"Jesus!" he screamed, "Spontaneous fucking combustion!"

All they found on the front seat of his car was a mound of ash.

Another Disgruntled Postal Employee

It wasn't easy always being the mail.

No matter the weather, the letters kept coming.

He looked silly in his uniform.

He hated sorting.

His world was split between the suits and unis.

He'd always be a uni and he knew it.

Then they told him he couldn't even be that.

He finally said: "I prefer to shoot you."

Next?

As the destruction of their world proceeds
From the great river forests they emerge,
Automatons, sub-microscopic, lethal,
Multiplying at exponential rates,

The viruses. Have we pressed to the verge
Some mechanism older than any evil?
If killing us is what the planet needs
It may be coded to exterminate.

Veronica

Car Phone

Technology's our world, and it's amazing.
The man in that car is talking on a phone.
Motion used to preclude communication.
It's not easy to talk to someone who keeps accelerating.

But the cords that bind us to places become outmoded.
We're all about maximum mobility.
And there's no need now to see anyone in person.
We can all keep in touch without ever leaving our cars.

In the beginning we were nomadic creatures.
And now at the end of the line we've come full circle.
This car I'm driving seems to know where it's going.
And I keep talking to you—hello, are you there?

Not You

Never there, you

It was all a myth, a myth all you

A woman reading.

Expanding as a gesture, you are large, ergo

Curled in the lamplight.

One foot on Nepal, the other on Peru, hand cupping the moon

Then leap into the Milky Way

Wrapping the words around her like a shawl.

Up the flashing eons, wherever you are

Her grandmother's shawl.

Wherever you are, where are you

In perfect sympathy.

America

You.

Not you

Letter

And if you can't come then

Nice here in May

Obligations of a professional nature.

Flowering birdsong

Cool in the evenings

Don't give us much time off for good behavior.

Or summer

Gin and tonics

Thunderstorms

That's one of our busiest seasons.

Or Nice in May

Henri Matisse

Climbing the orange streets

A view of the sea

Impossible to get away right now.

Time to go anywhere

No money to travel

I need a break but I can't get the time.

Scylla and Charybdis

As Shakespeare's Beatrice ruled any room
She turned on any speaker's careless phrase
And, in a carefree tone, lowered the boom.
They mumbled off in an embarrassed haze,
Or lingered to be cut up twenty ways
While the whole room had one long laughing fit.
That summer she was in her vicious phase.
Few came within the coiled reach of her wit
Who were not charmed by her, and then picked off by it.

The other swirled in circles as the moon
Kept changing faces in the summer sky.
She tugged, men came. Her sweet seductive tune
Mysteriously called each passer-by,
Each lover shone in her admiring eye.
(She kept the ring, the keys, the dressing gown—
She barely even knew it was a lie.)
Few tumbled in her arms who did not drown
In whirls of her confusion, down and down and down.

But here he hesitated. He could boast
A little self-control (or so he thought)
And so he steered his craft toward Scylla's coast.
Somehow she seemed exactly whom he sought:
They felt compatible, which really ought
To make things work. It *was* good, at the start.
It wasn't very long before they fought,
And then she picked his character apart
And plucked his ego, crying, from his open heart.

If somehow he survived (did he survive?)
It wasn't through his faith in one sure place
Where someone waited for him to arrive.

His old dissatisfaction with his face
Returned, and he resolved to quit the chase
To catch whatever beauty would appear
To turn men's heads and make their fool hearts race.
The choices that we face are rarely clear.
We make them out of pride, or selfishness, or fear.

Crossroads

What now?

It came to the point where he had to choose between irreconcilable ways of living.

How to remain free?

Ideals like freedom are irrelevant in the face of necessity.

No ideal, a visible space

A patch of sunlight on the hardwood floor

Local epiphanies do not address the exigencies of a professional society.

Only in such a place

Does the music occur

The attempt to live outside institutions may prove disastrous.

A gurgling in the furnace

A small voice

One might, for instance, be unable to afford health insurance.

The voices of the soul

The first law is to take care of yourself.

Shape's Horse

```
        the

            boy

                saw

            a           bright

S       H       A       P       E

            his         friend

S       H       A       P       E

            he      told    them

            they        laughed

            he      told    them

S       H       A       P       E

            had     a       horse

S       H       A       P       E'      S

                    H       O       R       S       E
```

The Prophet

He didn't really know what he was saying.
It was just patchwork, guesswork, shots in the dark.
Some guesses were educated, they all were wrong.
The future ducked his every calculation.

But he was condemned to have everyone believe him.
His mutterings were hailed as oracular truths.
Elaborate plans were keyed to his hints and inklings.
Catastrophe only enhanced his reputation.

Eventually he came to believe himself.
(This was his undoing, after he was dead.)
In the future, whatever would happen, he'd seen it coming.
That's what he said.

Adam

Adam had it good in Paradise.
He didn't have to work, there was plenty to eat.
He gave names to the things around him and that's what they were.
The woman was soft and sweet.

God said there were things he might as well not know.
That made him curious: the tree was forbidden, what for?
One day he felt like eating an apple, so he ate one.
He ate the skin and flesh, he ate the core.

For a moment there was perfect clarity.
He saw himself in relation to the world.
The names he had given to things were arbitrary.
His sense of his own importance was absurd.

And with that knowledge came a different freedom.
If words were false, one couldn't help but lie.
Soon everything in his head was one big lie.
He'd blame it all on Eve, Eve and the Devil.

He told that version to God and God believed it.
They both got punished for falling, but Eve got it worse.

He told it to her so often she almost believed it.
If she wasn't guilty, why did she keep getting hurt?

His narratives of deception grew more elaborate.
But Eden wasn't the best place for his art.
It was too pretty for words, the angels were watching.
He decided to leave the garden, to make a fresh start.

Eve didn't want to go, but he talked her into it.
Life on their own would be more full, more real.
But it had an emptiness Adam didn't anticipate.
There was nothing to violate, nothing to steal.

With no God to trick, his lies were pointless.
He needed language to organize the world.
He started naming again, as if he believed it.
As if there were such a thing as the literal word.

From that day forward his life was vaguely sad.
It was cold outside, for days it would rain.
Work was hard, Eve was under the weather.
The kids were fighting again.

Ivan Ho

My parents fell in love in Vladivostok
One winter half a century ago.
He was escaping war, she helped him go.
They had one night alone, that's all I took.

How I grew up, an orphan stealing food,
Finding a nook to sleep, stealing aboard
A freighter that delivered me abroad
Where I learned the local laws and learned them good,

Aping the foolish customs of the tribe,
Their dress and table habits, their odd taste
For food boiled to an indiscriminate paste,
How I became apprenticed to a scribe

Who taught me things I'll never tell a soul,
Incantatory charms to counter time
And ways to profit from fraternal crime,
Secrets that kill you, or just make you old,

How I stepped forth into the fractured world
Fearless because distracted, poor, and free,
And stood in the crowded marketplace, where she
Appeared in blue, a woman yet a girl,

Now elegant, now laughing easily,
How we talked for hours as the world walked by,
And said we'd tryst again, and kissed good-bye,
How I strolled on reciting breezily

But when I came to the appointed place
She wasn't there on time, she wasn't there,
Across the park the color of her hair
Entered a yellow cab, and with that trace

She vanished; how, then, stricken and possessed
By imperceptibly diminishing
Memories of her grace in some small thing,
I wandered in perpetual unrest

Through switchblade winds on ice-jammed polar seas,
Shivering at the giant sea-birds' screams,
Or twisted in the soft, delusive dreams
The endless desert conjures up to tease

The traveler, who wakes to stinging sand
And nothing more for miles of wind and sun,
How landscape after landscape came undone
Like tapestry unraveled by a hand

Laboring till a secret nighttime hour,
Unweaving all the lies the day had woven
To cover the long path the heart had chosen,
How finally a strange, forgetful power

Accrued around the pain, as I lost track
Of where I'd looked and where I hadn't been,
And couldn't tell, staring at any scene,
If it was new or I was doubling back,

How only then I found the spot I sought
Tucked in a corner of a steep ravine,
In miles of rock the one brush stroke of green,
Marked by the smoke ascending from her hut,

Why tell you, more than I already have?
You've got your story, just as I've got mine,
And could compare adventures line by line:
It starts with misdirection by a knave

Then sketches the essentials of your life,
Your banishment from the paternal home,

The futile war for Christendom and Rome
At epic distance from domestic strife,

Your masked return, humble in pilgrim's weeds,
Two lovely damsels with contrasting hair,
Your mortal feud with Brian de Bois-Guilbert . . .
But someone wrote your life to suit his needs

And your exploits were less than legendary:
You languished wounded more than half your novel
(Meanwhile the king was drinking in a hovel)
And Brian's death was very arbitrary.

Whatever ironies beset your tale,
They are of course nothing if not suspicious
Given the fact that everything's fictitious
When one's a character: your coat of mail

May flash like silver on a sunny day
But it's just tinsel, and a real broadsword
Will ribbon it if someone gives the word
To cut your story off and start a play.

Yet in such peril lies your true salvation:
A paper figure's almost light as air
So one strong wind can blow you anywhere
Within the compass of its inspiration,

And there's no telling where you'll be received,
Scattered like sparks and ashes from a fire
Or leaf-notes floating from the forest's lyre.
And though the quest may never be achieved

It must not be abandoned till the stage
When, finding that there's no grail to be found,
You hear a voice, like yours, but with a sound
In tune with something larger, like the age,

Or like your age, for by then you'll be old,
And you will see it wasn't what you sought
But how you sought it that resolved the plot
And let you rest at last, your long tale told

And added to the still progressing show.
So whether you're half Russian, half Chinese,
Or words cast spinning into play, like these,
The point's not who you are but how you know.

Fare forward traveler, and where you go
Tell them you saw Ivan, Ivan Ho.

Acknowledgments

The editor would like to thank *Boston Review* and *Western Humanities Review*, where some of these poems appeared, sometimes in slightly different form. "Frost Heaves" was published in Joseph Harrison's book *Someone Else's Name* (Waywiser, 2003), and is reprinted with permission of the author and the publisher.

About the Editor

J. H. Hobson is an editor, critic, and literary historian. His recent books include *The Worlds of Maurice Pomfret, The Mystery of Lisa Dell, The Reginald Gibbons Catastrophe,* and *Marko Stranski: An Evasion.* Among his many honors, he has twice received the Puttenham Medal from the Durham Institute of Poetics, and has been inducted into The Order of the Eagle by the Trustees of the Palacio Barolo. The Cambridge coachman Thomas Hobson, about whom Milton wrote two poems, is a distant ancestor. J. H. Hobson lives in Mexico.

www.ingramcontent.com/pod-product-compliance
Lightning Source LLC
LaVergne TN
LVHW091228080426
835509LV00009B/1209